The New Gospel of the Kingdom According to Saint Mark

The New Gospel of the Kingdom According to Saint Mark

Minister Bennie Earl Jenkins

Books Academy LLC
5900 Balcones Drive Suite 100
Austin, Texas 78731
Hotline: (254) 800-1183

Ordering Information:
Quantity sales. Special discounts are available on quantity purchases by corporations, associations, and others. For details, contact the publisher at the address above.

Printed in the United States of America.

ISBN-13:	Softcover	978-1-964864-31-0
	eBook	978-1-964864-32-7

Library of Congress Control Number: 2024915530

Table of Contents

Mark 1 1

Mark 2 5

Mark 3 8

Mark 4 11

Mark 5 15

Mark 6 19

Mark 7 24

Mark 8 27

Mark 9 30

Mark 10 34

Mark 11 39

Mark 12 42

Mark 13 46

Mark 14 49

Mark 15 55

Mark 16 59

About the Author 61

MARK 1

[1]   The beginning of the Gospel of King Yeshua, the Son of God;

[2]   As the prophets wrote in the scriptures, Behold, I send my messenger before thy face, which shall prepare thy way before thee.

[3]   The voice of one crying in the wilderness, Prepare ye the way of the Lord, make his paths straight.

[4]   John did baptize in the wilderness and preached the baptism of repentance for the remission of sins.

[5]   All the land of Judaea came out to him, and they of Jerusalem were all baptized of him in Jordan's river, confessing their sins.

[6]   And John clothed himself with camel's hair, and with a girdle of a skin about his loins; and he did eat locusts and wild honey;

[7]   John preached, saying, There comes one mightier than I after me, the latchet of whose shoes I am not worthy to stoop down and unloose.

[8]   I indeed have baptized you with water: but he shall baptize you with the Holy Ghost.

[9]   And it came to pass in those days, King Yeshua came from Nazareth of Galilee, and John baptized him in Jordan.

[10]   And straightway coming up out of the water, he saw the heavens opened, and the Spirit like a dove descending upon him:

[11] And there came a voice from heaven, saying, You are my beloved Son, in whom I am well pleased.

[12] And immediately, the Spirit drove him into the wilderness.

[13] And he was there in the wilderness forty days, tempted of Satan; and was with the wild beasts; and the angels ministered unto him.

[14] Now after that John was imprisoned, King Yeshua came into Galilee, preaching the gospel of the kingdom of God,

[15] And saying, The time is fulfilled, and the kingdom of God is at hand: repent, and believe the gospel.

[16] Now as he walked by the sea of Galilee, he saw Simon and Andrew his brother casting a net into the sea: for they were fishers.

[17] And King Yeshua, said unto them, Come ye after me, and I will make you fishers of men.

[18] And straightway they forsook their nets and followed him.

[19] And when he had gone a little further thence, he saw James, the Son of Zebedee, and John his brother, who also were in the ship mending their nets.

[20] And straightway he called them: and they left their Father Zebedee in the ship with the hired servants, and went after him.

[21] And they went into Capernaum, and straightway on the Sabbath day, he entered into the synagogue and taught.

[22] And they were astonished at his doctrine: for he taught them as one that had authority, and not as the scribes.

[23] And there was in their synagogue a man with an unclean spirit, and he cried out,

[24] Saying, Let us alone; what have we to do with thee, thou Yeshua of Nazareth? Have you come to destroy us? I know you who you are, the Holy One of God.

[25] And King Yeshua rebuked him, saying, Hold thy peace, and come out of him.

[26] And when the unclean spirit had torn him and cried with a loud voice, he came out of him.

[27] And they were all amazed, insomuch that they questioned among themselves, saying, What thing is this? what new doctrine is this? With authority, he commands even the unclean spirits, and they do obey him.

[28] And immediately his fame spread abroad throughout all the region round about Galilee.

[29] When they were come out of the synagogue, they entered into Simon and Andrew's house, with James and John.

[30] But Simon's wife's mother lay sick of a fever, and anon they tell him of her.

[31] And he came, took her by the hand, and lifted her; immediately, the fever left her, and she ministered unto them.

[32] And at sunset, they brought unto him all the diseased and those possessed with devils.

[33] And all the city assembled at the door.

[34] And he healed many who were sick of divers diseases, cast out many devils; and suffered not the devils to speak because they knew him.

[35] And in the morning, rising a great while before day, he went out and departed into a solitary place, and there prayed.

[36] And Simon and they that were with him followed after him.

[37] And when they had found him, they said unto him, All men seek for you.

[38] And he said unto them, Let us go into the next towns, that I may preach there also: for therefore came I forth.

[39] And he preached in their synagogues throughout all Galilee and cast out devils.

[40] And there came a leper to him, beseeching him, and kneeling to him, and saying unto him, If you will, you can make me clean.

[41] And King Yeshua moved with compassion, put forth his hand, and touched him, and saith unto him, I will; be thou clean.

[42] And as soon as he had spoken, immediately leprosy departed from him, and Our Father cleansed him.

[43] And he straitly charged him, and forthwith sent him away;

[44] And said unto him, See you say nothing to any man: but go your way, show yourself to the priest, and offer for thy cleansing those things which Moses commanded, for a testimony unto them.

[45] But he went out, began to publish it much, and blazed abroad the matter. Because King Yeshua could not openly enter into the city but stayed outside of it in desert places, they came to him from everywhere.

MARK 2

[1] And again, he entered into Capernaum, after some days; and people noised that he was in the house.

[2] And straightway, many people gathered together, insomuch that there was no room to receive them, no, not so much as about the door: and he preached the word unto them.

[3] And they came unto him, bringing one sick of the palsy, four bore him.

[4] And when they could not come nigh unto him for the press, they uncovered the roof where he was: opened it up, and they let down the bed wherein the sick of the palsy lay.

[5] When King Yeshua saw their faith, he said unto the sick of the palsy, Son, your sins be forgiven you.

[6] But there were certain of the scribes sitting there, and reasoning in their hearts,

[7] Why does this man thus speak blasphemies? Who can forgive sins but God only?

[8] And immediately when King Yeshua perceived in his spirit that they so reasoned within themselves, he said unto them, Why reason you these things in your hearts?

[9] Whether is it easier to say to the sick of the palsy, your sins be forgiven you; or to say, Arise, and take up your bed, and walk?

[10] But that you may know that the Son of man hath power on Earth to forgive sins, (he saith to the sick of the palsy,)

[11] I say unto you, Arise, take up your bed, and go your way into your house.

[12] And immediately he arose, took up the bed, and went forth before them all. They were all amazed and glorified God, saying, We never saw it in this fashion.

[13] And he went forth again by the seaside, and all the multitude resorted unto him, and he taught them.

[14] And as he passed by, he saw Levi the Son of Alphaeus sitting at the receipt of custom, and said unto him, Follow me. And he arose and followed him.

[15] And it came to pass, that, as King Yeshua sat at meat in his house, many publicans and sinners also sat together with King Yeshua and his disciples. Many followed him.

[16] And when the scribes and Pharisees saw him eat with publicans and sinners, they said unto his disciples, How is it that he eats and drinks with publicans and sinners?

[17] When King Yeshua heard it, he saith unto them, They that are whole do not need the physician, but they that are sick: I came not to call the righteous, but sinners to repentance.

[18] And the disciples of John and the Pharisees used to fast: and they come and say unto him, Why do the disciples of John and the Pharisees fast, but thy disciples fast not?

[19] And King Yeshua said unto them, Can the children of the bridechamber fast, while the bridegroom is with them? as long as they have the bridegroom with them, they cannot fast.

[20] But the days will come, when the bridegroom shall be taken away from them, and then shall they fast in those days.

[21] No man also sews a piece of new cloth on an old garment: else the new piece that filled it up taketh away from the old, and the rent is made worse.

[22] And no man puts new wine into old bottles: else the new wine doth burst the bottles, and the wine is spilled, and the bottles will be marred: but new wine must be put into new bottles.

[23] And it came to pass, that he went through the cornfields on the sabbath day; and his disciples began, as they went, to pluck the ears of corn.

[24] And the Pharisees said unto him, Behold, why do they on the Sabbath day that which is not lawful?

[25] And he said unto them, Have you never read what David did, when he had a need and was an hungered, he, and they that were with him?

[26] How he went into the house of God in the days of Abiathar, the high priest, and ate the shewbread, which is not lawful to eat. Only the priests could eat it. He also gave it to them which were with him?

[27] And he said unto them, The Sabbath was made for man, and not man for the Sabbath:

[28] Therefore the Son of man is Lord also of the sabbath.

MARK 3

[1] And he entered again into the synagogue, and there was a man there which had a withered hand.

[2] And they watched him, whether he would heal him on the Sabbath day; that they might accuse him.

[3] And he said unto the man who had the withered hand, Stand forth.

[4] And he said unto them, Is it lawful to do good on the Sabbath days or do evil? To save a life, or to kill? But they held their peace.

[5] And when he had looked round about on them with anger, he grieved for the hardness of their hearts. He said unto the man, stretch forth your hand. He stretched it out: and King Yeshua restored his hand whole like the other.

[6] And the Pharisees went forth, and straightway took counsel with the Herodians against him, how they might destroy him.

[7] But King Yeshua withdrew himself with his disciples to the sea: and a great multitude from Galilee followed him, and from Judaea,

[8] And from Jerusalem, and Idumaea, and from beyond Jordan; and they about Tyre and Sidon, a great multitude, when they had heard what great things he did, came unto him.

[9] And he spoke to his disciples, that a small ship should wait on him because of the multitude, lest they should throng him.

[10] For he had healed many; insomuch that they pressed upon him for to touch him, as many as had plagues.

[11] When they saw him, unclean spirits fell down before him and cried, saying, You are the Son of God.

[12] And he straitly charged them that they should not make him known.

[13] And he went up into a mountain, and called unto him whom he would: and they came unto him.

[14] And he ordained twelve, that they should be with him, and that he might send them forth to preach,

[15] And to have the power to heal sicknesses, and to cast out devils:

[16] And Simon he surnamed Peter;

[17] And James the Son of Zebedee, and John the brother of James; and he surnamed them Boanerges, which is, The sons of thunder:

[18] And Andrew, and Philip, and Bartholomew, and Matthew, and Thomas, and James the Son of Alphaeus, and Thaddaeus, and Simon the Canaanite,

[19] And Judas Iscariot, which also betrayed him: and they went into a house.

[20] And the multitude came together again so that they could not so much as eat bread.

[21] And when his friends heard of it, they went out to lay hold on him: for they said, He is beside himself.

[22] And the scribes which came down from Jerusalem said, He hath Beelzebub, and by the prince of the devils cast he out devils.

[23] And he called them unto him, and said unto them in parables, How can Satan cast out Satan?

[24] And if a kingdom is divided against itself, that kingdom cannot stand.

[25] And if a house is divided against itself, that house cannot stand.

[26] And if Satan rises up against himself, and be divided, he cannot stand, but hath an end.

[27] No man can enter into a strong man's house, and spoil his goods, except he will first bind the strong man; and then he will damage his home.

[28] Verily I say unto you, Our Father will forgive all sins unto the sons of men, and blasphemies wherewith soever they shall blaspheme:

[29] But he that shall blaspheme against the Holy Ghost shall never have forgiveness but is in danger of eternal damnation.

[30] Because they said, He hath an unclean spirit.

[31] Then came his brethren and his mother, and, standing without, sent unto him, calling him.

[32] And the multitude sat about him, and they said unto him, Behold, thy mother and thy brethren without seeking for thee.

[33] And he answered them, saying, Who is my mother, or my brethren?

[34] And he looked round about on them which sat about him, and said, Behold my mother and my brethren!

[35] For whosoever shall do the will of God, the same is my brother, and my sister, and mother.

MARK 4

[1] And he began again to teach by the seaside: and there was gathered unto him a great multitude. He entered into a ship and sat in the sea. The whole multitude stayed by the sea on the land.

[2] And he taught them many things by parables, and said unto them in his doctrine,

[3] Hearken; Behold, there went out a sower to sow:

[4] And it came to pass, as he planted, some fell by the wayside, and the fowls of the air came and devoured it up.

[5] And some fell on stony ground, where it had not much Earth; and immediately it sprang up because it had no depth of Earth:

[6] But when the sun was up, the sun-scorched it; and because it had no root, it withered away.

[7] And some fell among thorns, and the thorns grew up and choked it, and it yielded no fruit.

[8] And others fell on good ground, and did yield fruit that sprang up and increased; and brought forth, some thirty, some sixty, and some a hundred.

[9] And he said unto them, He that have ears to hear let him hear.

[10] And when he was alone, they were about him with the twelve asked of him the parable.

[11] He said unto them, It is given for you to know the mystery of the Kingdom of God: but they that are without will receive all these things in parables:

[12] That seeing they may see, and not perceive, and hearing they may hear, and not understand; lest at any time they should be converted, and their sins should be forgiven them.

[13] And he said unto them, Know ye not this parable? And how then will you know all parables?

[14] The sower soweth the word.

[15] These are they by the wayside, where the word is sown; but when they have heard, Satan comes immediately, and takes away the word that was sown in their hearts.

[16] And these are they likewise which are sown on stony ground; who, when they have heard the word, immediately receive it with gladness;

[17] And have no root in themselves, and so endure for a time: afterward, when affliction or persecution arises for the word's sake, immediately they are offended.

[18] And these are they which are sown among thorns; such as hear the word,

[19] And the cares of this world, and the deceitfulness of riches, and the lusts of other things entering in, choke the word, and it becometh unfruitful.

[20] And these are they which are sown on good ground; such as hear the word, receive it, and bring forth fruit, some thirtyfold, some sixty, and some a hundred.

[21] He said to them, Is a candle brought to put under a bushel, under a bed, and not set on a candlestick?

[22] For there is nothing hid, which shall not be manifested; neither was anything kept secret, but that it should come abroad.

[23] If any man has ears to hear, let him hear.

[24] And he said unto them, Take heed what you hear: with what measure you mete, it shall be measured to you: and unto you, that hear shall more be given.

[25] For he that hath, to him shall be given: and he that have not, from him shall be taken even that which he hath.

[26] And he said, So is the Kingdom of God, as if a man should cast seed into the ground;

[27] And should sleep rise night and day, and the seed should spring and grow up, he knows not how.

[28] For the Earth brings forth the fruit of herself; first the blade, then the ear, after that, the full corn in the ear.

[29] But when the fruit appears, immediately he puts in the sickle, because the harvest comes.

[30] And he said, Whereunto shall we liken the kingdom of God? or with what comparison shall we compare it?

[31] It is like a grain of mustard seed, when it is sown in the Earth, is less than all the seeds sown in the Earth:

[32] But when it is sown, it grows up, and becometh greater than all herbs, and shoots out great branches; so that the fowls of the air may lodge under the shadow of it.

[33] And with many such parables, he spoke the word unto them, as they could hear it.

[34] But without a parable, he did not speak unto them: and when they were alone, he expounded all things to his disciples.

[35] And the same day, when the even was come, he said unto them, Let us pass over unto the other side.

[36] And when they had sent away the multitude, they took him even as he was in the ship. And there were also with him other little ships.

[37] There arose a great storm of wind, and the waves beat into the ship so that it was now full.

[38] And he was in the hinder part of the ship, asleep on a pillow: and they awake him, and say unto him, Master, cares thou not that we perish?

[39] And he arose, and rebuked the wind, and said unto the sea, peace, be still. And the wind ceased, and there was a great calm.

[40] And he said unto them, Why are you so fearful? How is it that you have no faith?

[41] And they feared exceedingly, and said one to another, What manner of man is this, that even the wind and the sea obey him?

MARK 5

[1]   And they came over unto the other side of the sea, into the country of the Gadarenes.

[2]   When he stepped out of the ship, immediately He met a man out of the tombs with an unclean spirit,

[3]   Who had his dwelling among the tombs; and no man could bind him, no, not with chains:

[4]   Because they bound him often with fetters and chains, and the chains had been plucked asunder by him, and the fetters broken in pieces: neither could any man tame him.

[5]   And always, night and day, he was in the mountains, and in the tombs, crying, and cutting himself with stones.

[6]   But when he saw King Yeshua afar off, he ran and worshipped him,

[7]   And cried with a loud voice, and said, What have I to do with thee, King Yeshua thou Son of the highest God? I adjure thee by God that thou torment me not.

[8]   For he said unto him, Come out of the man, thou unclean spirit.

[9]   And he asked him, What is thy name? And he answered, saying, My name is Legion: for we are many.

[10]   And he begged him much that he would not send them away out of the country.

[11] Now there was there nigh unto the mountains a great herd of swine feeding.

[12] And all the devils begged him, saying, Send us into the swine, that we may enter into them.

[13] And forthwith King Yeshua gave them leave. And the unclean spirits went out, and entered into the swine: and the herd ran violently down a steep place into the sea, (they were about two thousand;) and sea choked in the sea.

[14] And they that fed the swine fled, and told it in the city, and in the country. And they went out to see what was done.

[15] And they come to King Yeshua, and see him that was possessed with the devil, and had the legion, sitting, and clothed, and in his right mind: and they were afraid.

[16] And they that saw it told them how it happened to him that was possessed with the devil and concerning the swine.

[17] And they began to pray him to depart out of their coasts.

[18] And when he came into the ship, he that devil possessed prayed him that he might be with him.

[19] Howbeit King Yeshua suffered him not, but said unto him, Go home to thy friends and tell them how great things the Lord hath done for thee, and hath had compassion on thee.

[20] And he departed and began to publish in Decapolis how great things King Yeshua had done for him: and all men did marvel.

[21] And when King Yeshua was passed over again by ship unto the other side, much people gathered unto him: and he was nigh unto the sea.

[22] And, behold, there came one of the rulers of the synagogue, Jairus by name; and when he saw him, he fell at his feet,

[23] And begged him intensely, saying, My little daughter lieth at the point of death and I pray thee, come and lay thy hands on her, that you heal her.; and she shall live.

[24] And King Yeshua went with him, and many people followed him and thronged him.

[25] And a certain woman, which had an issue of blood twelve years,

[26] And had suffered many things of many physicians, and had spent all that she had, and was nothing bettered, but rather grew worse,

[27] When she had heard of King Yeshua, came in the press behind, and touched his garment.

[28] For she said If I may touch but his clothes, I shall be whole.

[29] Straightway the fountain of her blood dried up, and she felt in her body that King Yeshua healed her of that plague.

[30] And King Yeshua, immediately knowing in himself that virtue had gone out of him, turned him about in the press, and said, Who touched my clothes?

[31] And his disciples said unto him, Do you see the multitude thronging thee, and sayest thou, Who touched me?

[32] And he looked round about to see her that had done this thing.

[33] But the woman fearing and trembling, knowing what happened in her, came and fell before him, and told him all the truth.

[34] And he said unto her, Daughter, thy faith hath made you whole; go in peace, and be whole of thy plague.

[35] While he yet spoke, there came from the ruler of the synagogue's house certain which said, your daughter is dead: why troubles thou the Master any further?

[36] As soon as King Yeshua heard the word that the servant spoke, he said unto the synagogue ruler, Be not afraid, only believe.

[37] And he suffered no man to follow him, save Peter, James, and John, the brother of James.

[38] He came to the house of the ruler of the synagogue and saw the tumult, and them that wept and wailed greatly.

[39] And when he came in, he said unto them, Why make you this ado, and weep? the Damsel is not dead but sleeps.

[40] And they laughed him to scorn. When he put them all out, he took the Father and the mother of the Damsel, and them with him, and entered in where the Damsel was lying.

[41] And he took the Damsel by the hand, and said unto her, Talitha cumi; which is, being interpreted, Damsel, I say unto thee, arise.

[42] And straightway, the Damsel arose and walked; for she was of the age of twelve years. And they were astonished with a great astonishment.

[43] And he charged them straitly that no man should know it; and commanded that something should be given her to eat.

MARK 6

[1] And he went out from thence and came into his own country, and his disciples follow him.

[2] And when the Sabbath day came, he began to teach in the synagogue: and many hearing him were astonished, saying, From whence hath this man these things? And what wisdom is this which is given unto him, that his hands wreak even such mighty works?

[3] Is not this the carpenter, the Son of Mary, the brother of James, and Joses, and of Juda, and Simon? and are not his sisters here with us? And they were offended at him.

[4] But King Yeshua said unto them, A prophet is not without honor, but in his own country, among his kin, and his own house.

[5] And he could there do no mighty work, save that he laid his hands upon a few sick folks, and healed them.

[6] And he marveled because of their unbelief. And he went round about the villages, teaching.

[7] And he called unto him the twelve, and began to send them forth by two and two, and gave them power over unclean spirits;

[8] And commanded them that they should take nothing for their journey, save a staff only; no scrip, no bread, no money in their purse:

[9] But be shod with sandals, and not put on two coats.

[10] And he said unto them, In what place soever you enter into a house, there abide till you depart from that place.

[11] And whosoever shall not receive you, nor hear you, when ye depart thence, shake off the dust under your feet for a testimony against them. Verily I say unto you. It shall be more tolerable for Sodom and Gomorrha in the day of judgment than for that city.

[12] And they went out and preached that men should repent.

[13] And they cast out many devils, anointed with oil many that were sick, and healed them.

[14] And King Herod heard of him; (for his name was spread abroad:) and he said, That John the Baptist rose from the dead, and therefore mighty works do show forth themselves in him.

[15] Others said That it is Elias. And others said, That it is a prophet, or as one of the prophets.

[16] But when Herod heard thereof, he said, It is John, whom I beheaded: he has risen from the dead.

[17] For Herod himself had sent forth and laid hold upon John, and bound him in prison for Herodias' sake, his brother Philip's wife: for he had married her.

[18] For John had said unto Herod, It is not lawful for thee to have thy brother's wife.

[19] Therefore Herodias quarreled with him and would have killed him, but she could not:

[20] For Herod feared John, knowing that he was a just man and a holy, and observed him; and when he heard him, he did many things, and heard him gladly.

[21] And when a convenient day was come, that Herod on his birthday made a supper to his lords, high captains, and chief estates of Galilee;

[22] And when the daughter of the said Herodias came in, and danced, and pleased Herod and them that sat with him, the King said unto the Damsel, Ask of me whatsoever thou wilt, and I will give it thee.

[23] And he sware unto her, Whatsoever thou shalt ask of me, I will give it you, unto the half of my kingdom.

[24] And she went forth, and said unto her mother, What shall I ask? And she said, The head of John the Baptist.

[25] And she came in straightway hastily unto the King, and asked, saying, I will that thou give me by and by in a charger the head of John the Baptist.

[26] And the King was exceeding sorry; yet for his oath's sake, and for their sakes which sat with him, he would not reject her.

[27] And immediately the King sent an executioner, and commanded his head to be brought: and he went and beheaded him in prison,

[28] Brought his head in a charger, and gave it to the Damsel: and the Damsel gave it to her mother.

[29] And when his disciples heard of it, they came, took up his corpse, and laid it in a tomb.

[30] And the apostles gathered themselves together unto King Yeshua, and told him all things, both what they had done, and what they had taught.

[31] And he said unto them, Come ye yourselves apart into a desert place, and rest a while: for there were many coming and going, and they had no leisure so much as to eat.

[32] And they departed into a desert place by ship privately.

[33] And the people saw them departing, and many knew him, ran afoot thither out of all cities, outwent them, and came together unto him.

[34] And King Yeshua, when he came out, saw much people, and was moved with compassion toward them because they were as sheep not having a shepherd: and he began to teach them many things.

[35] And when the day ended for them, his disciples came unto him, and said, This is a desert place, and now the time is far passed:

[36] Send them away, that they may go into the country round about, and into the villages, and buy themselves bread: for they have nothing to eat.

[37] He answered and said unto them, Give you them to eat. And they say unto him, Shall we go and buy two hundred pennyworths of bread, and give them to eat?

[38] He said unto them, How many loaves have you? Go and see. And when they knew, they say, Five, and two fishes.

[39] And he commanded them to make all sit down by companies upon the green grass.

[40] And they sat down in ranks, by hundreds, and by fifties.

[41] And when he had taken the five loaves and the two fishes, he looked up to heaven, and blessed, and brake the loaves, and gave them to his disciples to set before them. The two fishes divided them among them all.

[42] And they did all eat and were filled.

[43] And they took up twelve baskets full of the fragments, and of the fishes.

[44] And they that did eat of the loaves were about five thousand men.

[45] And straightway, he constrained his disciples to get into the ship and go to the other side before unto Bethsaida, while he sent away the people.

[46] And when he had sent them away, he departed into a mountain to pray.

[47] When even was come, the ship was in the midst of the sea, and he alone on the land.

[48] He saw them toiling in rowing. The wind was contrary unto them. And the night came unto them about the fourth Watch. He came to them, walking upon the sea, and would have passed by them.

[49] But when they saw him walking upon the sea, they supposed it had been a spirit, and cried out:

[50] For they all saw him and were troubled. And immediately he talked with them, and said unto them, Be of good cheer: it is I; be not afraid.

[51] And he went up unto them into the ship, and the wind ceased: they were sore amazed in themselves beyond measure and wondered.

[52] For they considered not the miracle of the loaves: for they hardened hearts.

[53] And when they had passed over, they came into the land of Gennesaret, and drew to the shore.

[54] And when they were come out of the ship, straightway they knew him,

[55] And ran through that whole region round about, and began to carry about in beds those that were sick, where they heard he was.

[56] And whithersoever he entered, into villages, or cities, or country, they laid the sick in the streets and begged him that they might touch if it were, but the border of his garment: and as many as touched him were made whole.

MARK 7

[1] Then came together unto him the Pharisees, and certain of the scribes, which came from Jerusalem.

[2] And when they saw some of his disciples eat bread with defiled, that is to say; they found fault with unwashed hands.

[3] For the Pharisees and all the Jews, except they wash their hands oft, eat not, holding the elders' tradition.

[4] And when they come from the market, except they wash, they eat not. And many other things there be, which they have received to hold, as the washing of cups, pots, brazen vessels, and tables.

[5] Then the Pharisees and scribes asked him, Why walk not thy disciples according to the tradition of the elders, but eat bread with unwashed hands?

[6] He answered and said unto them, Well hath Esaias prophesied of you hypocrites. As it is written, these people honoureth me with their lips, but their heart is far from me.

[7] Howbeit in vain do they worship me, teaching for doctrines the commandments of men.

[8] For laying aside the commandment of God, ye hold the tradition of men, as the washing of pots and cups: and many other such like things you do.

[9] And he said unto them, Full well ye reject the commandment of God, that ye may keep your own tradition.

[10] For Moses said, Honour thy Father and thy mother; and, Whoso curseth father or mother, let him die the death:

[11] But you say, If a man shall say to his Father or mother, It is Corban, that is to say, a gift, by whatsoever thou mightest be profited by me; he shall be free.

[12] And you suffer him no more to do ought for his Father or his mother;

[13] Making the word of God of none effect through your tradition, which you have delivered: and many such like things do you.

[14] And when he had called all the people unto him, he said unto them, Hearken unto me every one of you, and understand:

[15] There is nothing from without a man that entering into him can defile him: but the things that come out of him are those that defile the man.

[16] If any man has ears to hear, let him hear.

[17] And when he entered into the house from the people, his disciples asked him concerning the parable.

[18] And he saith unto them, Are you so without understanding also? Do you not perceive, that whatsoever thing from without entereth into the man, it cannot defile him;

[19] Because it entereth not into his heart, but the belly, and goes out into the draught, purging all meats?

[20] And he said That which cometh out of the man, that defileth the man.

[21] For from within, out of the heart of men, proceed evil thoughts, adulteries, fornications, murders,

[22] Thefts, covetousness, wickedness, deceit, lasciviousness, an evil eye, blasphemy, pride, foolishness:

[23] All these evil things come from within and defile the man.

[24] And from thence, he arose, went into the borders of Tyre and Sidon, entered into a house, and would have no man know it: but he could not be hidden.

[25] For a certain woman, whose young daughter had an unclean spirit, heard of him, and came and fell at his feet:

[26] The woman was a Greek, a Syrophenician by nation; and she begged him to cast forth the devil out of her daughter.

[27] But King Yeshua said unto her, Let the children first be filled: it is not meet to take the children's bread and cast it unto the dogs.

[28] And she answered and said unto him, Yea, Lord: yet the dogs under the table eat of the children's crumbs.

[29] And he said unto her, For this saying go thy way; the devil is gone out of thy daughter.

[30] And when she came to her house, she found the devil gone out, and her daughter laid upon the bed.

[31] And again, departing from the coasts of Tyre and Sidon, he came unto the sea of Galilee, through the midst of the coasts of Decapolis.

[32] And they bring unto him one that was deaf and had an impediment in his speech, and they beseech him to put his hand upon him.

[33] And he took him aside from the multitude and put his fingers into his ears, and he spit and touched his tongue;

[34] And looking up to heaven, he sighed, and said unto him, Ephphatha, that is, Be opened.

[35] And straightway his ears opened, and the string of his tongue was loosed, and he spake plain.

[36] And he charged them that they should tell no man: but the more he charged them, so much the more a great deal they published it;

[37] The people were beyond measure astonished, saying, He hath done all things well: he maketh both the deaf to hear and the dumb to speak.

MARK 8

[1] In those days the multitude being very great, and having nothing to eat, King Yeshua called his disciples unto him, and saith unto them,

[2] I have compassion for the multitude because they have now been with me three days and have nothing to eat:

[3] And if I send them away fasting to their own houses, they will faint by the way: for divers of them came from far.

[4] And his disciples answered him, From whence, can a man satisfy these men with bread here in the wilderness?

[5] And he asked them, How many loaves have you? And they said, Seven.

[6] And he commanded the people to sit down on the ground: and he took the seven loaves, and gave thanks, and brake, and gave to his disciples to set before them, and they did set them before the people.

[7] And they had a few small fishes: and he blessed, and commanded to set them also before them.

[8] So they did eat, and were filled: and they took up the broken meat that was left seven baskets.

[9] And they that had eaten were about four thousand: and he sent them away.

[10] And straightway, he entered into a ship with his disciples and came into the parts of Dalmanutha.

[11] And the Pharisees came forth and began to question with him, seeking of him a sign from heaven, tempting him.

[12] And he sighed deeply in his Spirit, and said, Why does this generation seek after a sign? Verily I say unto you; there shall no sign be given unto this generation.

[13] And he left them and entering into the ship again departed to the other side.

[14] Now the disciples had forgotten to take bread, neither had they in the ship with them more than one loaf.

[15] And he charged them, saying, Take heed, beware of the leaven of the Pharisees, and of the leaven of Herod.

[16] And they reasoned among themselves, saying, It is because we have no bread.

[17] And when King Yeshua knew it, he said unto them, Why reason ye, because you have no bread? Perceive you not yet, neither understand? have you your heart yet hardened?

[18] Having eyes, see you not? And having ears, hear you not? And do you not remember?

[19] When I brake the five loaves among five thousand, how many baskets full of fragments took ye up? They say unto him, Twelve.

[20] And when the seven among four thousand, how many baskets full of fragments took ye up? And they said, Seven.

[21] And he said unto them, How is it that ye do not understand?

[22] And he came to Bethsaida, and they bring a blind man unto him, and begged him to touch him.

[23] And he took the blind man by the hand, and led him out of the town; and when he had spit on his eyes and put his hands upon him, he asked him if he saw ought.

[24] And he looked up, and said, I see men as trees, walking.

[25] After that, he put his hands again upon his eyes and made him look up: and he was restored, and saw every man.

[26] And he sent him away to his house, saying, Neither go into the town nor tell it to any in the town.

[27] And King Yeshua went out, and his disciples, into the towns of Caesarea Philippi: and by the way he asked his disciples, saying unto them, Who do men say that I am?

[28] And they answered, John the Baptist: but some say, Elias; and others, One of the prophets.

[29] And he said unto them, But whom say you that I am? And Peter answereth and said unto him, Thou art the Christ.

[30] And he charged them that they should tell no man of him.

[31] And he began to teach them that the Son of man must suffer many things, be rejected of the elders, and of the chief priests, scribes, and be killed, and after three days rise again.

[32] And he spake that saying openly. And Peter took him and began to rebuke him.

[33] But when he had turned about and looked on his disciples, he rebuked Peter, saying, Get thee behind me, Satan: for thou savourest not the things that be of God, but the things that be of men.

[34] And when he had called the people unto him with his disciples, he said unto them; Whosoever will come after me, let him deny himself, take up his cross, and follow me.

[35] For whosoever will save his life shall lose it; but whosoever shall lose his life for my sake and the gospel's, the same shall save it.

[36] For what shall it profit a man if he shall gain the whole world and lose his own soul?

[37] Or what shall a man give in exchange for his soul?

[38] Whosoever, therefore, shall be ashamed of me and my words in this adulterous and sinful generation. The Son of man shall be ashamed of him when he cometh in the glory of his Father with the holy angels.

MARK 9

[1]   And he said unto them, Verily I say unto you, That some of them standing here, shall not taste of death, till they have seen the kingdom of God come with power.

[2]   And after six days King Yeshua took with him Peter, and James, and John, and leadeth them up into a high mountain apart by themselves: and he was transfigured before them.

[3]   And his raiment became shining, exceeding white as snow; so as no fuller on Earth can white them.

[4]   And there appeared unto them Elias with Moses: and they were talking with King Yeshua.

[5]   And Peter answered and said to King Yeshua, Master, it is good for us to be here: and let us make three tabernacles; one for thee, and one for Moses, and one for Elias.

[6]   For he wist not what to say; for they were sore afraid.

[7]   And there was a cloud that overshadowed them: and a voice came out of the cloud, saying, This is my beloved Son: hear him.

[8]   And suddenly, when they had looked round about, they saw no man any more, save King Yeshua only with themselves.

[9]   And as they came down from the mountain, he charged them that they should tell no man what things they had seen, till the Son of man had risen from the dead.

[10] And they kept that saying with themselves, questioning one with another what the rising from the dead should mean.

[11] And they asked him, saying, Why say the scribes that Elias must first come?

[12] And he answered and told them, Elias verily came first, and restored all things; and how it is written of the Son of man, he must suffer many things, and be set at naught.

[13] But I say unto you, That Elias is indeed come, and they have done unto him whatsoever they listed, as it is written of him.

[14] And when he came to his disciples, he saw a great multitude about them, and the scribes questioning them.

[15] And straightway all the people, when they beheld him, were greatly amazed, and running to him saluted him.

[16] And he asked the scribes, What question you with them?

[17] And one of the multitudes answered and said, Master, I have brought unto you my Son, which hath a dumb spirit;

[18] And wheresoever he took him, he tore him: and he foamed, and gnashed with his teeth, and pineth away: and I spake to your disciples that they should cast him out, and they could not.

[19] He answered him, and said, O faithless generation, how long shall I be with you? How long shall I suffer you? Bring him unto me.

[20] And they brought him unto him: and when he saw him, straightway the spirit tare him; and he fell on the ground, and wallowed foaming.

[21] And he asked his father, How long is it ago since this came unto him? And he said, Of a child.

[22] And ofttimes it hath cast him into the fire, and into the waters, to destroy him: but if you canst do anything, have compassion on us, and help us.

[23] King Yeshua said unto him, If you can believe, all things are possible to him that believes.

[24] And straightway, the father of the child cried out, and said with tears, Lord, I believe; help you mine unbelief.

[25] When King Yeshua saw that the people came running together, he rebuked the foul spirit. Saying unto him, you dumb and deaf spirit, I charge you, come out of him, and enter no more into him.

[26] And the spirit cried, and rent him sore, and came out of him: and he was as one dead; insomuch that many said, he is dead.

[27] But King Yeshua took him by the hand, and lifted him up, and he arose.

[28] And when he came into the house, his disciples asked him privately, Why could not we cast him out?

[29] And he said unto them; this kind can come forth by nothing, but by prayer and fasting.

[30] And they departed thence and passed through Galilee, and he wished that no man should know it.

[31] For he taught his disciples, and said unto them, The Son of man is delivered into the hands of men, and they shall kill him; and after that he is killed, he shall rise the third day.

[32] But they understood not that saying and were afraid to ask him.

[33] And he came to Capernaum: and being in the house, he asked them, What was it that you disputed among yourselves by the way?

[34] But they held their peace: for by the way they had disputed among themselves, who should be the greatest.

[35] And he sat down and called the twelve, and saith unto them, If any man desire to be first, the same shall be last of all, and servant of all.

[36] And he took a child, and set him in the midst of them: and when he had taken him in his arms, he said unto them,

[37] Whosoever shall receive one of such children in my name, receives me: and whosoever shall receive me, receives not me, but him that sent me.

[38] And John answered him, saying, Master, we saw one casting out devils in thy name, and he does not follow us: and we forbad him because he does not follow us.

[39] But King Yeshua said, Forbid him not: for there is no man which shall do a miracle in my name, that can lightly speak evil of me.

[40] For he, that is not against us is on our part.

[41] For whosoever shall give you a cup of water to drink in my name because you belong to Christ, verily I say unto you, he shall not lose his reward.

[42] And whosoever shall offend one of these little ones that believe in me; it is better for him that someone hang a millstone about his neck, and cast him into the sea.

[43] And if your hand offend thee, cut it off: it is better for thee to enter into life maimed than having two hands to go into hell, into the fire that never shall be quenched:

[44] Where their worm dies not, and the fire is not quenched.

[45] And if your foot offends you, cut it off: it is better for thee to enter halt into life, than having two feet to be cast into hell, into the fire that never shall be quenched:

[46] Where their worm dies not, and the fire is not quenched.

[47] And if your eye offends thee, pluck it out: it is better for thee to enter into the kingdom of God with one eye than having two eyes to be cast into hell fire:

[48] Where their worm dieth not, and the fire is not quenched.

[49] For every one shall be salted with fire, and every sacrifice shall be salted with salt.

[50] Salt is good: but if the salt has lost his saltness, wherewith will ye season it? Have salt in yourselves, and have peace one with another.

MARK 10

[1] And he arose from there, and came into the coasts of Judaea by the farther side of Jordan: and the people resort unto him again; and, as he was wont, he taught them also.

[2] And the Pharisees came to him and asked him, Is it lawful for a man to put away his wife? Tempting him.

[3] And he answered and said unto them, What did Moses command you?

[4] And they said Moses suffered to write a bill of divorcement and to put her away.

[5] And King Yeshua answered and said unto them, For the hardness of your heart he wrote you this precept.

[6] But from the beginning of the creation, God made them male and female.

[7] For this cause shall a man leave his father and mother, and cleave to his wife;

[8] And they twain shall be one flesh: so then they are no more twain, but one flesh.

[9] What therefore God hath joined together, let not man put asunder.

[10] And in the house, his disciples asked him again of the same matter.

[11] And he saith unto them, Whosoever shall put away his wife, and marry another, committeth adultery against her.

[12] And if a woman shall put away her husband, and be married to another, she committeth adultery.

[13] And they brought young children to him, that he should touch them: and his disciples rebuked those that brought them.

[14] But when King Yeshua saw it, he was much displeased, and said unto them, Suffer the little children to come unto me, and forbid them not: for of such is the kingdom of God.

[15] Verily I say unto you; whosoever shall not receive the kingdom of God as a little child, he shall not enter therein.

[16] And he took them up in his arms, put his hands upon them, and blessed them.

[17] And when he was gone forth into the way, there came one running, and kneeled to him, and asked him, Good Master, what shall I do that I may inherit eternal life?

[18] And King Yeshua said unto him, Why call you me good? There is none good but one, that is, God.

[19] Thou knowest the commandments, Do not commit adultery, Do not kill, Do not steal, Do not bear false witness, Defraud not, Honour thy father and mother.

[20] And he answered and said unto him, Master, all these have I observed from my youth.

[21] Then King Yeshua beholding him loved him, and said unto him, One thing thou lackest: go thy way, sell whatsoever thou hast, and give to the poor, and thou shalt have treasure in heaven: and come, take up the cross, and follow me.

[22] And he was sad at that saying and went away grieved: for he had great possessions.

[23] And King Yeshua looked round about, and saith unto his disciples, How hardly shall they that have riches enter into the kingdom of God!

[24] And the disciples were astonished at his words. But King Yeshua answereth again, and saith unto them, Children, how hard is it for them that trust in riches to enter into the kingdom of God!

[25] It is easier for a camel to go through the eye of a needle, than for a rich man to enter into the kingdom of God.

[26] And they were astonished out of measure, saying among themselves, Who then can be saved?

[27] And King Yeshua looking upon them saith, With men, it is impossible, but not with God: for with God all things are possible.

[28] Then Peter began to say unto him, Lo, we have left all, and have followed you.

[29] And King Yeshua answered and said, Verily I say unto you, no man hath left the house, or brethren, or sisters, or father, or mother, or wife, or children, or lands, for my sake, and the gospels,

[30] But he shall receive a hundredfold now in this time, houses, and brethren, and sisters, and mothers, and children, and lands, with persecutions; and in the world to come eternal life.

[31] But many that are first shall be last; and the last first.

[32] And they were in the way going up to Jerusalem, and King Yeshua went before them: and they were amazed; and as they followed, they were afraid. And he took again the twelve, and began to tell them what things should happen unto him,

[33] Saying, Behold, we go up to Jerusalem; and the Son of man shall be delivered unto the chief priests, and unto the scribes. They shall condemn him to death, and shall deliver him to the Gentiles:

[34] And they shall mock him, and shall scourge him, and shall spit upon him, and shall kill him: and the third day he shall rise again.

[35] And James and John, the sons of Zebedee, come unto him, saying, Master, we would like for thou shouldest do for us whatsoever we shall desire.

[36] And he said unto them, What would you that I should do for you?

[37] They said unto him, Grant unto us that we may sit, one on thy right hand, and the other on thy left hand, in thy glory.

[38] But King Yeshua said unto them; you know not what you ask: can you drink of the cup that I drink of? And be baptized with the baptism that I am baptized with?

[39] And they said unto him, We can. And King Yeshua said unto them, You shall indeed drink of the cup that I drink of; and with the baptism that I am baptized withal shall you be baptized:

[40] But to sit on my right hand and on my left hand is not mine to give; but it shall be given to them for whom it is prepared.

[41] And when the ten heard it, they began to be much displeased with James and John.

[42] But King Yeshua called them to him, and saith unto them, You know that they which are accounted to rule over the Gentiles exercise lordship over them. Their great ones exercise authority upon them.

[43] But so shall it not be among you: but whosoever will be great among you, shall be your minister:

[44] And whosoever of you will be the chiefest, shall be the servant of all.

[45] For even the Son of man came not to be ministered unto, but to minister and give his life a ransom for many.

[46] And they came to Jericho: and as he went out of Jericho with his disciples and a great number of people, blind Bartimaeus, the Son of Timaeus, sat by the highway side begging.

[47] And when he heard that it was King Yeshua of Nazareth, he began to cry out, and say, King Yeshua, thou Son of David, have mercy on me.

[48] And many charged him that he should hold his peace: but he cried the more a great deal, Thou Son of David, have mercy on me.

[49] And King Yeshua stood still and commanded him to be called. And they call the blind man, saying unto him, Be of good comfort, rise; he calleth thee.

[50] And he, casting away his garment, rose, and came to King Yeshua.

[51] And King Yeshua answered and said unto him, What will you that I should do unto thee? The blind man said unto him, Lord, that I might receive my sight.

[52] And King Yeshua said unto him, Go your way; your faith hath made thee whole. And immediately he received his sight and followed King Yeshua in the way.

MARK 11

[1] And when they came nigh to Jerusalem, unto Bethphage and Bethany, at the Mount of Olives, he sendeth forth two of his disciples,

[2] And said unto them, Go your way into the village over against you: and as soon as ye enter into it, ye shall find a colt tied, whereon never man sat; loose him, and bring him.

[3] And if any man says unto you, Why do you this? say you that the Lord hath need of him; and straightway he will send him hither.

[4] And they went their way and found the colt tied by the door without in a place where two ways met, and they loose him.

[5] And certain of them that stood there said unto them, What do ye, loosing the colt?

[6] And they said unto them even as King Yeshua had commanded: and they let them go.

[7] And they brought the colt to King Yeshua, and cast their garments on him, and he sat upon him.

[8] And many spread their garments in the way: and others cut down branches off the trees, and strawed them in the way.

[9] And they that went before, and they that followed, cried, saying Hosanna; Blessed is he that cometh in the name of the Lord:

[10] Blessed be the kingdom of our Father David, that cometh in the name of the Lord: Hosanna in the highest.

[11] King Yeshua entered into Jerusalem, and the temple. When he looked round about upon all things, and now the eventide came, he went out unto Bethany with the twelve.

[12] And on the morrow, when they came from Bethany, he was hungry:

[13] He saw a fig tree afar off having leaves, he came, if haply he might find anything thereon. When he came to it, he found it had nothing but leaves; for the time of figs was not yet.

[14] And King Yeshua answered and said unto it, No man eat the fruit of thee hereafter forever. And his disciples heard it.

[15] And they come to Jerusalem: and King Yeshua went into the temple, and began to cast out them that sold and bought in the temple, and overthrew the tables of the moneychangers, and the seats of them that sold doves;

[16] And would not suffer that any man should carry any vessel through the temple.

[17] And he taught, saying unto them, Is it not written, My house shall be called of all nations the house of prayer? But ye have made it a den of thieves.

[18] And the scribes and chief priests heard it, and sought how they might destroy him: for they feared him because all the people was astonished at his doctrine.

[19] And when even was come, he went out of the city.

[20] And in the morning, they saw the fig tree dried up from the roots as they passed by.

[21] And Peter calling to remembrance said unto him, Master, behold, the fig tree which thou cursed is withered away.

[22] And King Yeshua answering said unto them, Have faith in God.

[23] For verily I say unto you, That whosoever shall say unto this mountain, Be thou removed, and be thou cast into the sea. And shall not doubt in his heart, but shall believe that those things he said shall come to pass; he shall have whatsoever he saith.

[24] Therefore I say unto you, What things soever you desire when you pray, believe that you receive them, and you shall have them.

[25] And when you stand praying, forgive, if ye have ought against any: that your Father also which is in heaven may forgive you your trespasses.

[26] But if you do not forgive, neither will your Father which is in heaven forgive your trespasses.

[27] And they come again to Jerusalem: and as he was walking in the temple, there come to him the chief priests, and the scribes, and the elders,

[28] And say unto him, By what authority do you these things? And who gave thee this authority to do these things?

[29] And King Yeshua answered and said unto them, I will also ask of you one question, and answer me, and I will tell you by what authority I do these things.

[30] The baptism of John, was it from heaven, or of men? Answer me.

[31] And they reasoned with themselves, saying, If we shall say, From heaven; he will say, Why then did you not believe him?

[32] But if we shall say, Of men; they feared the people: for all men counted John, that he was a prophet indeed.

[33] And they answered and said unto King Yeshua, We cannot tell. And King Yeshua answering saith unto them, Neither do I tell you by what authority I do these things.

MARK 12

[1]   And he began to speak unto them by parables. A certain man planted a vineyard, set a hedge about it, dug a place for the winefat, built a tower, let it out to husbandmen, and went into a far country.

[2]   And at the season he sent to the husbandmen a servant, that he might receive from the husbandmen of the vineyard's fruit.

[3]   And they caught him, and beat him, and sent him away empty.

[4]   And again he sent unto them another servant; at him, they cast stones, wounded him in the head, and sent him away shamefully handled.

[5]   And again he sent another, and him they killed, and many others; beating some, and killing some.

[6]   Therefore, having yet one Son, his well-beloved, he sent him also last unto them, saying, They will reverence my Son.

[7]   But those husbandmen said among themselves, This is the heir; come, let us kill him, and the inheritance shall be ours.

[8]   And they took him, and killed him, and cast him out of the vineyard.

[9]   What shall therefore the Lord of the vineyard do? he will come and destroy the husbandmen and will give the vineyard unto others.

[10]   And have you not read this scripture; The stone which the builders rejected has become the head of the corner:

[11] This work was the Lord's doing, and it is marvelous in our eyes?

[12] And they sought to lay hold on him but feared the people: for they knew that he had spoken the parable against them: and they left him, and went their way.

[13] And they send unto him certain of the Pharisees and of the Herodians, to catch him in his words.

[14] When they came, they say unto him, Master, we know that thou art true, and carest for no man. For thou regardest not the person of men, but teachest the way of God in truth: Is it lawful to give tribute to Caesar, or not?

[15] Shall we give, or shall we not give? But he, knowing their hypocrisy, said unto them, Why tempt ye me? Could you bring me a penny, that I may see it?

[16] And they brought it. And he saith unto them, Whose is this image and superscription? And they said unto him, Caesar's.

[17] And King Yeshua answering said unto them, Render to Caesar the things that are Caesar's, and to God the things that are God's. And they marveled at him.

[18] Then come unto him the Sadducees, which say there is no resurrection; and they asked him, saying,

[19] Master, Moses wrote unto us, If a man's brother dies, leave his wife behind him, and leave no children, that his brother should take his wife, and raise seed unto his brother.

[20] Now there were seven brethren: and the first took a wife, and dying left no seed.

[21] And the second took her, and died, neither left he any seed: and the third likewise.

[22] And the seven had her, and left no seed: last of all the woman died also.

[23] Therefore, in the resurrection, when they shall rise, whose wife shall she be of them? for the seven had her to wife.

[24] And King Yeshua answering said unto them, Do you not, therefore, error, because you know not the scriptures, neither the power of God?

[25] When they shall rise from the dead, they neither marry nor are given in marriage; but are as the angels in heaven.

[26] And as touching the dead, that they rise: have you not read in the book of Moses, how in the bush God spake unto him, saying, I am the God of Abraham, and the God of Isaac, and the God of Jacob?

[27] He is not the God of the dead, but the God of the living: ye, therefore, greatly error.

[28] And one of the scribes came and having heard them reasoning together, and perceiving that he had answered them well, asked him, Which is the first commandment of all?

[29] And King Yeshua answered him, The first of all the commandments is, Hear, O Israel; The Lord our God is one Lord:

[30] And thou shalt love the Lord thy God with all thy heart, and with all thy soul, and with all thy mind, and with all thy strength: this is the first commandment.

[31] And the second is like, namely this, Thou shalt love thy neighbor as thyself. There is no other commandment greater than these.

[32] And the scribe said unto him, Well, Master, thou hast said the truth: for there is one God; and there is none other but he:

[33] And one must love him with all the heart, and with all the understanding, and with all the soul, and with all the strength and love his neighbor as himself. This is more than all whole burnt offerings and sacrifices.

[34] And when King Yeshua saw that he answered discreetly, he said unto him, you art not far from the kingdom of God. And no man after that durst asks him any question.

[35] And King Yeshua answered and said, while he taught in the temple, How say the scribes that Christ is the Son of David?

[36] For David himself said by the Holy Ghost, The Lord said to my Lord, Sit thou on my right hand, till I make your enemies thy footstool.

[37] David, therefore, himself calleth him Lord; and why is he then his Son? And the ordinary people heard him gladly.

[38] And he said unto them in his doctrine, Beware of the scribes, which love to go in long clothing, and love salutations in the marketplaces,

[39] And the chief seats in the synagogues, and the uppermost rooms at feasts:

[40] Which devour widows' houses, and for a pretense make long prayers: these shall receive greater damnation.

[41] And King Yeshua sat over against the treasury. He beheld how the people cast money into the treasury: and many that were rich cast in much.

[42] And there came a certain poor widow, and she threw in two mites, making a farthing.

[43] And he called unto him his disciples, and said unto them, Verily I say unto you, That this poor widow hath cast more in, than all they which have cast into the treasury:

[44] For all they did cast in of their abundance; but she of her want did cast in all that she had, even all her living.

MARK 13

[1] And as he went out of the temple, one of his disciples said unto him, Master, see what manner of stones and buildings are here!

[2] And King Yeshua answering said unto him, Seest thou these great buildings? There shall not be left one stone upon another, that shall not be thrown down.

[3] And as he sat upon the mount of Olives over against the temple, Peter and James and John and Andrew asked him privately,

[4] Tell us, when shall these things be? And what sign shall tell us when all these things shall be fulfilled?

[5] And King Yeshua answering them began to say, Take heed lest any man deceive you:

[6] For many shall come in my name, saying, I am Christ; and shall deceive many.

[7] And when ye shall hear of wars and rumors of wars, be ye not troubled: for such things must need to be; but the end shall not be yet.

[8] For nation shall rise against nation, and kingdom against kingdom: and there shall be earthquakes in divers places, and there shall be famines and troubles: these are the beginnings of sorrows.

[9] But take heed to yourselves: for they shall deliver you up to councils; and in the synagogues ye shall be beaten: and ye shall be brought before rulers and kings for my sake, for a testimony against them.

[10] And the gospel must first be published among all nations.

[11] But when they shall lead you, and deliver you up, take no thought beforehand what you shall speak, neither do you premeditate: but whatsoever shall be given you in that hour, that speak you: for it is not you that speaks, but the Holy Ghost.

[12] Now the brother shall betray the brother to death, and the Father the Son; and children shall rise up against their parents and cause them to be put to death.

[13] And all men hate you for my name's sake: but he that shall endure unto the end, the same shall be saved.

[14] But when you shall see the abomination of desolation, spoken of by Daniel the prophet, standing where it ought not, (let him that readeth understand,) then let them that be in Judaea flee to the mountains.

[15] And let him that is on the housetop not go down into the house, neither enter therein, to take any thing out of his house:

[16] And let him that is in the field not turn back again for to take up his garment.

[17] But woe to them that are with child, and to them that give suck in those days!

[18] And pray you that your flight is not in the winter.

[19] For in those days shall be affliction, such as was not from the beginning of the creation God created unto this time, neither shall be.

[20] And except that the Lord had shortened those days, no flesh should be saved: but for the elect's sake, whom he hath chosen, he hath shortened the days.

[21] And then if any man shall say to you, Lo, here is Christ; or, lo, he is there; believe him not:

[22] For false Christs and false prophets shall rise, and shall show signs and wonders, to seduce, if it were possible, even the elect.

[23] But take ye heed: behold, I have foretold you all things.

[24] But in those days, after that tribulation, the sun shall be darkened, and the moon shall not give her light,

[25] And the stars of heaven shall fall, and the powers that are in heaven shall be shaken.

[26] And then shall they see the Son of man coming in the clouds with great power and glory.

[27] And then shall he send his angels and gather together his elect from the four winds, from the uttermost part of the Earth to the uttermost part of heaven.

[28] Now learn a parable of the fig tree; When her branch is yet tender, and putteth forth leaves, ye know that summer is near:

[29] So ye in like manner when ye shall see these things come to pass, know that it is nigh, even at the doors.

[30] Verily I say unto you, that this generation shall not pass until all these things are done.

[31] Heaven and Earth shall pass away: but my words shall not pass away.

[32] That day and that hour no man knows, no, not the angels in heaven, neither the Son, but the Father.

[33] Take you heed, watch and pray: for you know not when the time is.

[34] For the Son of man is a man taking a far journey, who left his house, gave authority to his servants, and to every man his work, and commanded the porter to watch.

[35] Watch you therefore: for you know not when the Master of the house cometh, at even, or at midnight, or the cockcrowing, or in the morning:

[36] Lest coming suddenly, he finds you sleeping.

[37] And what I say unto you I say unto all, Watch.

MARK 14

[1] After two days was the feast of the Passover, and unleavened bread: and the chief priests and the scribes sought how they might take him by craft, and put him to death.

[2] But they said, Not on the feast day, lest there be an uproar of the people.

[3] And being in Bethany in Simon's house, the leper, as he sat at meat, there came a woman having an alabaster box of ointment of spikenard very precious. She broke the box and poured it on his head.

[4] And some had indignation within themselves, and said, Why was this waste of the ointment made?

[5] It might have been sold for more than three hundred pence and have been given to the poor. And they murmured against her.

[6] And King Yeshua said, Let her alone; why trouble you her? she have wrought a good work on me.

[7] For you have the poor with you always, and whensoever you will you may do them good: but me ye have not always.

[8] She hath done what she could: she is come aforehand to anoint my body to the burying.

[9] Verily I say unto you, Wheresoever this gospel shall be preached throughout the whole world. This work that she hath done shall also be spoken of for a memorial of her.

[10] And Judas Iscariot, one of the twelve, went unto the chief priests, to betray him unto them.

[11] And when they heard it, they were glad and promised to give him money. And he sought how he might conveniently betray him.

[12] And the first day of unleavened bread, when they killed the Passover, his disciples said unto him, Where wilt thou that we go and prepare that thou mayest eat the Passover?

[13] And he sendeth forth two of his disciples, and saith unto them, Go ye into the city, and there shall meet you a man bearing a pitcher of water: follow him.

[14] And wheresoever he shall go in, say ye to the goodman of the house, The Master saith, Where is the guest-chamber, where I shall eat the Passover with my disciples?

[15] And he will show you a large upper room furnished and prepared: there make ready for us.

[16] And his disciples went forth, and came into the city, and found as he had said unto them: and they made ready the Passover.

[17] And in the evening he cometh with the twelve.

[18] And as they sat and did eat, King Yeshua said, Verily I say unto you, One of you which eateth with me shall betray me.

[19] And they began to be sorrowful, and to say unto him one by one, Is it I? and another said, Is it I?

[20] And he answered and said unto them, It is one of the twelve, that dips with me in the dish.

[21] The Son of man indeed goeth, as it is written of him: but woe to that man by whom the Son of man is betrayed! It is good for that man if he had never been born.

[22] And as they did eat, King Yeshua took bread, blessed, broke it, gave to them, and said, Take, eat: this is my body.

[23] And he took the cup, and when he had given thanks, he gave it to them: and they all drank of it.

[24] And he said unto them; this is my blood of the new testament, which I shed for many.

[25] Verily I say unto you, I will drink no more of the fruit of the vine, until that day that I drink it new in the kingdom of God.

[26] And when they had sung a hymn, they went out into the Mount of Olives.

[27] And King Yeshua saith unto them, All ye shall be offended because of me this night: for it is written, I will smite the shepherd, and the sheep shall be scattered.

[28] But after that I rise, I will go before you into Galilee.

[29] But Peter said unto him, Although all shall be offended, yet will not I.

[30] And King Yeshua said unto him, Verily I say unto you, That this day, even in this night, before the cock crow twice, thou shalt deny me thrice.

[31] But he spake the more vehemently, If I should die with thee, I will not deny thee in any wise. Likewise also said they all.

[32] And they came to a place named Gethsemane: and he said to his disciples, Sit you here, while I shall pray.

[33] And he taketh with him Peter and James and John, and began to be sore amazed, and to be very heavy;

[34] And He said unto them, My soul is exceeding sorrowful unto death: tarry ye here and watch.

[35] And he went forward a little, and fell on the ground, and prayed that, if it were possible, the hour might pass from him.

[36] And he said, Abba, Father, all things are possible unto you; take away this cup from me: nevertheless not what I will, but what you will.

[37] And he cometh, and findeth them sleeping, and saith unto Peter, Simon, sleepest thou? Couldest, not thou watch one hour?

[38] Watch ye and pray, lest ye enter into temptation. The Spirit indeed is ready, but the flesh is weak.

[39] And again he went away and prayed, and spake the same words.

[40] And when he returned, he found them asleep again, (for their eyes were heavy,) neither wist they what to answer him.

[41] And he came the third time, and said unto them, Sleep on now, and take your rest: it is enough, the hour has come; behold, the Son of man is betrayed into the hands of sinners.

[42] Rise let us go; lo, he that betrays me is at hand.

[43] And immediately, while he yet spake, cometh Judas, one of the twelve, and with him a great multitude with swords and staves, from the chief priests and the scribes and the elders.

[44] And he that betrayed him had given them a token, saying, Whomsoever I shall kiss, that same is he; take him and lead him away safely.

[45] And as soon as he came, he goeth straightway to him, and said, Master, Master; and kissed him.

[46] And they laid their hands on him and took him.

[47] And one of them stood by drew a sword, smote a servant of the high priest, and cut off his ear.

[48] And King Yeshua answered and said unto them, Are you come out, as against a thief, with swords and with staves to take me?

[49] I was daily with you in the temple teaching, and ye took me not: but the scriptures must be fulfilled.

[50] And they all forsook him and fled.

[51] And there followed him a certain young man, having a linen cloth cast about his naked body; and the young men laid hold on him:

[52] And he left the linen cloth and fled from them naked.

[53] And they led King Yeshua away to the high priest: and with him were assembled all the chief priests and the elders and the scribes.

[54] And Peter followed him afar off, even into the high priest's palace: and he sat with the servants, and warmed himself at the fire.

[55] And the chief priests and all the council sought witness against King Yeshua to put him to death; and found none.

[56] For many bare false witness against him, but their witness agreed not together.

[57] And there arose certain, and bare false witness against him, saying,

[58] We heard him say, I will destroy this temple that is made with hands, and within three days, I will build another made without hands.

[59] But neither so did their witness agree together.

[60] And the high priest stood up in the midst, and asked King Yeshua, saying answer thou nothing? What is it which these witness against thee?

[61] But he held his peace and answered nothing. Again the high priest asked him, and said unto him, Art thou the Christ, the Son of the Blessed?

[62] And King Yeshua said, I am: and you shall see the Son of man sitting on the right hand of power, and coming in the clouds of heaven.

[63] Then the high priest rent his clothes, and said, What need we any further witnesses?

[64] You have heard the blasphemy: what think you? And they all condemned him to be guilty of death.

[65] And some began to spit on him, and to cover his face, and to buffet him. They said unto him, Prophesy: and the servants did strike him with the palms of their hands.

[66] And as Peter was beneath in the palace, there came one of the maids of the high priest:

[67] And when she saw Peter warming himself, she looked upon him, and said, And you also wast with Yeshua of Nazareth.

[68] But he denied, saying, I know not, neither understand I what you sayest. And he went out into the porch; and the cock crew.

[69] And a maid saw him again and began to say to them that stood by. This man is one of them.

[70] And he denied it again. And a little after, they that stood by said again to Peter, Surely you are one of them: for you are a Galilaean, and your speech agrees to it.

[71] But he began to curse and to swear, saying, I know not this man of whom you speak.

[72] And the second time, the cock crew. And Peter called to mind the word that King Yeshua said unto him, Before the cock crow twice, thou shalt deny me thrice. And when he thought thereon, he wept.

MARK 15

[1] And straightway in the morning the chief priests held a consultation with the elders and scribes and the whole council, and bound King Yeshua, and carried him away, and delivered him to Pilate.

[2] And Pilate asked him, Are you the King of the Jews? And he answering said unto him; you said it.

[3] And the chief priests accused him of many things: but he answered nothing.

[4] And Pilate asked him again, saying, Answerest you nothing? Behold how many things they witness against thee.

[5] But King Yeshua yet answered nothing; so that Pilate marveled.

[6] Now at that feast, he released unto them one prisoner, whomsoever they desired.

[7] And there was one named Barabbas, which lay bound with them that had made insurrection with him, who had murdered in the insurrection.

[8] And the multitude crying aloud began to desire him to do as he had ever done unto them.

[9] But Pilate answered them, saying, Will ye that I release unto you the King of the Jews?

[10] For he knew that the chief priests had delivered him for envy.

[11] But the chief priests moved the people, that he should instead release Barabbas unto them.

[12] And Pilate answered and said again unto them, What will you then that I shall do unto him whom you call the King of the Jews?

[13] And they cried out again, Crucify him.

[14] Then Pilate said unto them, Why, what evil hath he done? And they cried out the more exceedingly, Crucify him.

[15] And so Pilate, willing to content the people, released Barabbas unto them, and delivered King Yeshua, when he had scourged him, to be crucified.

[16] And the soldiers led him away into the hall, called Praetorium; and they call together the whole band.

[17] And they clothed him with purple, and platted a crown of thorns, and put it about his head,

[18] And began to salute him, Hail, King of the Jews!

[19] And they smote him on the head with a reed, and did spit upon him, and bowing their knees worshipped him.

[20] And when they had mocked him, they took off the purple from him, and put his clothes on him, and led him out to crucify him.

[21] And they compel one Simon a Cyrenian, who passed by, coming out of the country, the Father of Alexander and Rufus, to bear his cross.

[22] And they bring him unto the place Golgotha, which is, being interpreted, The place of a skull.

[23] And they gave him to drink wine mingled with myrrh: but he received it not.

[24] And when they had crucified him, they parted his garments, casting lots upon them, what every man should take.

[25] And it was the third hour, and they crucified him.

[26] And the superscription of his accusation was written over, The King of the Jews.

[27] They crucified two thieves with him, the one on his right hand, and the other on his left.

[28] And the scripture was fulfilled, which saith, And he was numbered with the transgressors.

[29] And they that passed by railed on him, wagging their heads, and saying, Ah, you that destroys the temple, and builds it in three days,

[30] Save yourself, and come down from the cross.

[31] Likewise also the chief priests mocking said among themselves with the scribes, He saved others; himself he cannot save.

[32] Let Christ the King of Israel descend now from the cross, that we may see and believe. And they that were crucified with him reviled him.

[33] And when the sixth hour came, there was darkness over the whole land until the ninth hour.

[34] And at the ninth hour, King Yeshua cried with a loud voice, saying, Eloi, Eloi, lama sabachthani? Which is, being interpreted, My God, my God, why hast thou forsaken me?

[35] And some of them that stood by, when they heard it, said, Behold, he calleth Elias.

[36] And one ran and filled a sponge full of vinegar, and put it on a reed, and gave him to drink, saying, Let alone; let us see whether Elias will come to take him down.

[37] And King Yeshua cried with a loud voice and gave up the ghost.

[38] And the veil of the temple was rent in twain from top to bottom.

[39] And when the centurion, which stood over against him, saw that he so cried out, and gave up the ghost, he said, Truly this man was the Son of God.

[40] There were also women looking on afar off: among whom was Mary Magdalene, and Mary the mother of James the Less and Joses, and Salome;

[41] (Who also, when he was in Galilee, who followed him and ministered unto him;) and many other women who came up with him unto Jerusalem.

[42] And now when the even was come, because it was the preparation, that is, the day before the sabbath,

[43] Joseph of Arimathaea, an honorable counselor who also waited for the kingdom of God, came in boldly unto Pilate and craved the body of King Yeshua.

[44] And Pilate marveled if he were already dead: and calling unto him the centurion, he asked him whether he had been any while dead.

[45] And when he knew it of the centurion, he gave the body to Joseph.

[46] And he bought fine linen, and took him down, and wrapped him in the linen, and laid him in a tomb which was hewn out of a rock, and rolled a stone unto the door of the tomb.

[47] And Mary Magdalene and Mary the mother of Joses beheld where he was laid.

MARK 16

[1]   And when the sabbath was past, Mary Magdalene, and Mary, James and Salome's mother, had bought sweet spices, that they might come and anoint him.

[2]   And very early in the morning, the first day of the week, they came unto the tomb at the rising of the sun.

[3]   And they said among themselves, Who shall roll away the stone from the door of the tomb for us?

[4]   And when they looked, they saw that the stone was rolled away: for it was enormous.

[5]   And entering into the tomb, they saw a young man sitting on the right side, clothed in a long white garment; and the young man frightened.

[6]   And he saith unto them, Be not afraid: You seek Yeshua of Nazareth, which was crucified: he has risen; he is not here: behold the place where they laid him.

[7]   But go your way, tell his disciples and Peter that he goeth before you into Galilee: there shall ye see him, as he said unto you.

[8]   And they went out quickly, and fled from the tomb; for they trembled and were amazed: neither said they anything to any man; for they were afraid.

[9]   Now when King Yeshua rose early the first day of the week, he appeared first to Mary Magdalene, out of whom he had cast seven devils.

[10] And she went and told them that had been with him, as they mourned and wept.

[11] When they had heard that he was alive and had been seen of her, they believed not.

[12] After that, he appeared in another form unto two of them, as they walked, and went into the country.

[13] And they went and told it unto the residue: neither did they believe them.

[14] Afterward, he appeared unto the eleven as they sat at meat and upbraided them with their unbelief and hardness of heart. Because they believed not them which had seen him after he rose.

[15] And he said unto them, Go ye into all the world, and preach the gospel to every creature.

[16] He that believes and is baptized shall be saved, but he that believeth not shall be damned.

[17] And these signs shall follow them that believe; In my name shall they cast out devils; they shall speak with new tongues;

[18] They shall take up serpents; and if they drink any deadly thing, it shall not hurt them; they shall lay hands on the sick, and they shall recover.

[19] So then, after the King Yeshua had spoken unto them, he was received up into heaven and sat on the right hand of God.

[20] And they went forth, and preached everywhere, the Lord working with them, and confirming the word with signs following. Amen.

ABOUT THE AUTHOR

In fall 2020, the Holy Spirit inspired Minister Bennie Earl Jenkins to produce this work to bring honor, respect, and reverence to the name of our Savior. Brother Jenkins was born again and baptized at an early age. He has served in many capacities in the church over years. He has served as a deacon, Sunday-school teacher, trustee, usher, and musician. He answered the call to the ministry in the fall of 2019.

Minister Jenkins was born in 1950 in Livingston, Texas, to Oscar B. Jenkins and Carrie L. Bogany. He grew up as a member of a family of eight children in Hardin County, Texas, and did exceptionally well in school. Benny was always a responsible young man who took an active role in caring for his younger brothers and sisters. His mother raised him in the church under strict guidance; he studied several religions and attended various churches before adopting his ministry.

When he graduated from high school, Benny was accepted for enrollment in Lamar University in Beaumont, Texas; he maintained a job while attending college, which he used to help pay for his educational expenses. After completing his bachelor's degree in chemistry, he obtained employment with a large chemical company. Minister Jenkins has four daughters and a grandson.

While working in the chemical industry, Minister Jenkins obtained a master's degree in chemistry and became a certified industrial hygienist

(CIH). Upon leaving the chemical industry, he became a health protection administrator for a large school district. Benny later accepted a job as a professor of chemistry in the Department of Chemistry at a community college. He has worked at the community college for the last twenty-five years. He has achieved recognition as a distinguished professor of chemistry. Fishing and golfing are his hobbies. His favorite charity is Feed the Children.

You can view his program every Sabbath at 3:00 PM on the King Yeshua Ministries YouTube channel.

www.ingramcontent.com/pod-product-compliance
Lightning Source LLC
Chambersburg PA
CBHW051553120626
46551CB00013B/1501